D1157662

# Still with God

# Still with God

## finding quiet in the chaos

## SUE McCORMACK

credo
house publishers

*Still with God*
Copyright © 2022 by Sue McCormack
All rights reserved.

Published in the United States of America by Credo House Publishers,
a division of Credo Communications LLC, Grand Rapids, Michigan
credohousepublishers.com

Unless otherwise indicated, Scripture quotations are taken from
the Holy Bible, New International Version®, NIV®.
Copyright © 1973, 1978, 1984, 2011 by Biblica, Inc.™
Used by permission of Zondervan. All rights reserved worldwide.

ISBN: 978-1-62586-240-2

Cover and interior design and layout by Sharon VanLoozenoord
Editing by Elizabeth Banks

*Printed in the United States of America*
First edition

# Still with God

# SITTING STILL

*Be still, and know that I am God.*

PSALM 46:10

When I was growing up and my mom and dad would say "Let's go!" we would bound out the door, jump in the back seat, and immediately ask, "Where are we goin'?" My mom always replied, "Sit still and ride Clyde." After asking the same question a hundred more times, my dad would say something funny like "There and back again to see how far it was" or "See ya around Newt's barn." Let me just say, I have no idea who Newt is or how to get to his barn. I have discovered as an adult that I had undiagnosed ADHD as a child and sitting still was a major undertaking for me.

Have you ever had trouble sitting still? Do you have a tough time turning off your mind? Are you easily distracted by phone calls, text messages, calendars, sports practice, kids, laundry, dinner, work, spouse? There are a million things that pull us in that many directions daily. I am fifty-four years old and still struggle, but in the last few years I have found who helps me "sit still." It is God.

My most favorite verse in the Bible is Psalm 46:10: "Be still, and know that *I am God*" (emphasis added). There is something about this verse that resonates daily with me. God wants us to be still with Him, to be present with Him. I have said God is not going to shout or scream at us, or even thump us on the head; that is too easy. No, being still forces us to seek Him, to hear Him, and to be present with Him. He is available for us, always. We have His undivided attention and presence every time we ask for it.

It makes me feel special when someone takes the time to give me their undivided attention. Imagine how our Lord God feels when we give Him ours? Take time every day this week to be still with God, finding a "still spot" where you can be undistracted and focused. You might be surprised how much you will begin to look forward to being still with Him daily. I promise you it will become the best part of your day!

## 𝒫RAYER FOR THIS WEEK

*Father God, help me to be still with You*
*each day so I can hear Your still small voice.*
*Teach me to be present and undistracted with You.*
*Thank You for loving me and listening to me*
*even when I am not being still.*
*In Jesus's name, amen.*

# SHEMA

*"Which is the most important [commandment]?"*
*"The most important one," Jesus answered "is this:*
*'Hear, O Israel: The Lord our God, the Lord is one. Love*
*the Lord your God with all your heart and with all your*
*soul and with all your mind and with all your strength.'*
*The second is this: 'Love your neighbor as yourself.'*
*There is no commandment greater than these."*

DEUTERONOMY 6:4–5

Put your Hebrew history hat on and let's unpack the Shema a little bit! I have a passion for Jewish culture and religion. *Shema* spoken in Hebrew is beautiful. "Sh'ma Yisra'eil Adonai Eloheinu Adonai echad." "Hear, Israel, the Lord is our G-d, the Lord is One."

Beautiful right? Are you wondering why the "o" is missing? Traditionally, the name of G-d was considered so sacred by the Hebrews that it was not spelled out in print form. This attempt to give His name the highest respect and reverence, by omitting any vowels, also helped them avoid having to erase or destroy the holy name of G-d. Other names were often used in its place, such as "the Merciful One," "the Creator," "our King." Some Jews also use G!d to show enthusiasm for God and Judaism.

It gives us something to think about when we carelessly use His name in spoken or written word. The third of the Ten Commandments in Exodus 20:7 reads: "You shall not misuse the name of the LORD your God, for the LORD will not hold anyone guiltless who misuses his name." I get frustrated if someone spells my name wrong. It's always spelled wrong. McCorm-Ick. Now I say it's McCorm-Ack with an "A" not Ick with an "I."

I'm nobody and I get frustrated over misspelling my name. Imagine how the Lord God, our Creator and sustainer must feel when we are careless with His most precious name. One of my favorite hymns is "There's Just Something About That Name." "Jesus, Jesus, Jesus, let all heaven and earth proclaim, kings and kingdoms will all pass away, but there's something about that name." Don't forget who you belong to! Yes, I am a prince or a princess. My Father is the King of Kings!

### $\mathscr{P}$RAYER FOR THIS WEEK

*Jesus, never let me forget that Your name*
*is above all names, and to always be careful*
*to speak lovingly and respectfully when I share*
*about You and Your precious name.*
*In Jesus's name, amen.*

# DNA

*I will be a Father to you, and you will be*
*my sons and daughters, says the Lord Almighty.*
2 CORINTHIANS 6:18

When I was seven years old my mom met my dad. The math doesn't add up, I know, and that's because he wasn't my biological father. The memories that I have from my first seven years aren't very good. My biological father was an alcoholic, a womanizer, and abusive to my mom, my older sister, my younger brother, and myself. I remember things were very scary a lot of times because you never knew what would set him off. Silly stuff, like we were not allowed to walk in front of the television if he was watching it; we had to crawl on our hands and knees across the floor so he wouldn't miss anything. When my mom would go to work, he would lock us out of the house and tell us to use the bathroom underneath the porch.

There was a lot of screaming at my mom and at us. My mom would try to shield us from it, but we were all in the crosshairs. He was a miserable, angry, unhappy man who blamed everyone else for his lot in life, especially us. The turning point finally came when my mom filed for divorce. He was so angry. He was served the papers at work. When he got off, he came to the house, knocked my mom down, and started choking her. We were terrified because we thought he was going to kill her. It all happened so fast, and by the grace of God he left.

And that was the only example we knew, as children, of how a man relates to his wife and children. At seven years old I was sure I didn't want a husband or a dad, but that all changed for us. My mom started dating a man named Don, who treated her with respect and love—something we had never seen before. He was divorced and had four kids of his own. And the way he treated us? He treated us like we were his kids! It wasn't long before we asked if we could call him "Dad." He said whatever we wanted was okay with him, so Dad it was. It blew me away how he made us feel like we were his kids. "Step" was never part of his title or ours. "This is my dad." "This my daughter." Wow! I belonged to someone who says I am his daughter! As time went on, I always said "my dad" or "my brother and sisters"; I never felt that they were anything else but my siblings.

The Lord Almighty knew I needed Him and my dad (see this week's theme verse). He sent the man who showed us how a dad loves not hurts, builds up not tears down, sees us as his. There are not a lot of men who would take on three more kids and build a life and legacy filled with so much love. He was there and present for everything big and small; to walk all five daughters down the aisle, encouraging his sons on their wedding days, ball games, dances, proms, births, reunions, picnics, Christmases, Thanksgivings, birthdays, and so much more! I may not have his physical DNA, but I have his values of love, integrity, honor, and respect. I am who I am today because the Lord showed me what a father, who is created in His image, is supposed to be and I'm so grateful for that. My dad took his last breath on earth and his first breath in heaven on June 12, 2009, after a hard-fought battle with COPD.

### 𝒫RAYER FOR THIS WEEK

*Thank You, heavenly Father, for being the Dad*
*You knew we needed and letting us experience*
*good fathers here on earth. Help us learn*
*what Your good father's heart toward us is like.*
*In Jesus's name, amen.*

# I DON'T WANT TO

*Bear with each other and forgive one another*
*if any of you has a grievance against someone.*
*Forgive as the Lord forgave you.*

COLOSSIANS 3:13

I had already made up my mind that I would not forgive my biological father for all the things he did to us. He doesn't deserve it. I realized early on that we were never important to him. He would see us for a while then disappear back down whatever bottle he was drinking. It came to an awful head when I was twelve or thirteen. He wanted to take us to Kings Island amusement park. I thought to myself, *okay. He's footing the bill. Go and have a good time.* My sister and her boyfriend drove us there along with my brother, myself, and Alfred (that's what we called him, by his name).

We mostly did our own thing and agreed to meet at a spot near the concession stands. When we met up, he was sitting at a table drinking a beer. By the look of the empty beer cups, he was buzzing. He made an inappropriate remark to a teenage girl there and we were like, "Nope. Get up; we're leaving!" We were mortified. We had to stop for gas, and he had to go to the bathroom. I told my sister, "Let's leave him there." She said, "No, we can't do that." We waited for him in the car, and he came back with what else but a twelve-pack of beer. I was fuming!

You see, he had just gotten out of rehab a few days before. If he could spend money on us (buy our love), we'd give him a pass. But *nope!* I lost it on him. I said things to him that I wish I could say I was ashamed of, but at the time it felt right. Honestly it felt good. His response was typical: "I don't know how to be a father. Your mother this . . . your grandmother that . . ." And he saved his best excuse for last: he "drinks because of us" . . . Wow! Everyone else is the reason he *chose* to drink.

We didn't see him for a few years after that. I was totally okay with that. I got married when I was eighteen and pregnant, to a guy who was, ironically, just like Alfred. His addiction was marijuana and sex. He, too, was abusive. I stayed way longer than I should have—less than four years, but it seemed like a lifetime. I divorced him, but the abuse continued verbally. He was stalking me and threatening to kill me; it was awful. I realized history was repeating itself. I was living a page from my mother's book, and I sadly accepted that this was the "love" I thought I deserved

Then the best thing happened to me—I met the love of my life, Dale. God sent him to me to bring me back to God. He was exactly what I needed in my life, a godly man. He read the Bible daily and invited me to study with him. The rest is history. We have been married for twenty-eight years and have been together twenty-nine years. Dale is a man like my dad, Don. Because my dad showed true love to my mom and us, I was able to happily accept the real love I truly deserved from Dale.

After many devotionals together, it seemed like every one was about forgiveness. Ugh! I would go through the motions thinking it doesn't apply to me or my situation. But then one day God really got my attention. The Scripture for the day was Colossians 3:13, as seen above. Ouch! Along with this verse was teaching that made so much sense. Forgiveness is not something that is always easy and sometimes we don't want to forgive. Instead we need to pray for the will to forgive, and when it becomes your prayer, forgiveness eventually follows. I can attest that it does.

It had been several years since I had spoken to Alfred, but I woke up one morning with an urgency to talk to him. So I did. I went to his apartment, and it wasn't what I expected. When he saw me, after years mind you, all he said was, "What do you want?" I told him, "Nothing. I just wanted you to know that I don't hate you and I forgive you." Before I knew what was coming out of my mouth next, I had already said it. I asked him to forgive me too. He said, "Is that it?" I said, "Yes." He turned around and walked away like he was unfazed. I, however, was set free when I walked away. Carrying all that around was like carrying a sack of bricks. The very moment I forgave him, I set that bag down, never to pick it back up again!

Are you weighed down by the sack of bricks called unforgiveness? Don't let it become so heavy it cripples you. Pray for the will to forgive. God hears you and He loves you!

### *P*RAYER FOR THIS WEEK

*Lord, help us to want Your will in our lives*
*and please give us the will to forgive those*
*who hurt us even when we don't want to.*
*In Jesus's name, amen.*

# BENCHWARMER
# OR TEAM PLAYER?

*Do not think that because you are in the king's house*
*you alone of all the Jews will escape. For if you remain silent*
*at this time, relief and deliverance for the Jews will arise*
*from another place, but you and your father's family will*
*perish. And who knows but that you have come*
*to your royal position for such a time as this?*

ESTHER 4:13-14

Benchwarmer or team player? Which one are you? How often are we happy to sit on the sidelines and watch; or are you the one that rallies the team and leads them to victory? I wasn't athletically inclined as a kid in organized sports, but I did like to watch. Sometimes I even got picked to be on a team with my friends. I wanted to be good at a sport, but I often sat on the bench. Basketball was not for me. It was like everyone knew who was good and who wasn't. So I never got the ball or the glory.

I discovered major league baseball and learned to play in church league softball. I loved it! I wasn't great at it, but I played with heart and enthusiasm. Also, I did enjoy the smack talk and heckling from the bench, probably way too much. I realized that even if I wasn't in the game, I still was an important part of team. I was cheering for my team and encouraging them to keep going. I was finally good at something related to sports. One day after a game, the coach said to me, "What you're doing from the bench is just as important as running the bases and hitting home runs. Thanks for being part of the team." Well after that I never really cared if I was on the bench or in the game, I was still part of team. That's what I was there for.

Esther had a dilemma on her hands. When Mordecai found out about Haman's plan to kill the Jews, he went to Esther and asked her to help. Esther was a Jew, and she was also the queen. But even though she was the queen, she couldn't walk up to the king whenever she wanted. To do so could get her killed. The king had to extend his gold scepter to accept her. She sent word to Mordecai telling him what would happen if she approached the king. Mordecai sent his response, as seen in this week's theme passage.

Esther sent back instructions for all the Jews to be gathered in Susa and to fast for three days and nights. When the fast was over she would go to the king, even though it was against the law. She was willing to risk death for her people.

God used Esther to help save her people from certain death at the hands of Haman, who was put to death on the king's orders. She was on the bench, but when her time came, she was the ultimate team player. Don't be afraid of what God has brought you to in this moment of your life. You are here for such a time as this!

## $\mathcal{P}$RAYER FOR THIS WEEK

*Father God, thank You for creating us
for such a time as this and may we always be
ready to get off the bench when it's time.
In Jesus's name, amen.*

# HIDDEN POTENTIAL OR UNDERACHIEVER?

*Do you not know? Have you not heard?*
*The Lord is the everlasting God,*
*the Creator of the ends of the earth.*
*He will not grow tired or weary,*
*and his understanding no one can fathom.*
*He gives strength to the weary*
*and increases the power of the weak.*
*Even youths grow tired and weary,*
*and young men stumble and fall;*
*but those who hope in the Lord*
*will renew their strength.*
*They will soar on wings like eagles;*
*they will run and not grow weary;*
*they will walk and not be faint.*

ISAIAH 40:28-31

I heard a story about a college football player who was a senior and played fullback. His coach and teammates considered him to be a goof-off because he was never serious. They never saw him play up to his potential. One day during homecoming week they were out on the practice field, and he received a message that his father had passed away. He immediately left and went to be with his family for his father's funeral.

He returned on game day. The stadium was packed to capacity. The crowd's roar was like thunder as they ran out of the tunnel. The game started and they played hard, but his team was losing by thirteen points with four minutes left in the game. The goof-off went to the coach and asked him if he could play. The coach thought for a second and said "Why not, you're a senior. You've never played up to your potential, we're losing, and you can't hurt us. Go on in."

He ran out on the field and played like a man on fire! He went out to the line and ran through the defense like it was nothing and scored. There was an onside kick, and they got the ball and gave it to him again and he ran like a bulldozer over the other team. They kicked the extra point and won the game!

In the locker room the coach asked him, "What in the world got into you? You have had tremendous potential the last four years but never wanted to reach it, and then today we got to see how good you are! Why?" He said, "Coach you know my dad died this week, and my dad was a Christian. What you didn't know is that my dad was blind and never saw me play in a football game. Today I knew my dad would be watching from heaven and I wanted to run my very best and play up to my full potential so my dad would be proud."

Even when we have days that we put in half the effort, or days when we don't want to at all, and figure who cares if I don't do everything up to my full potential, God cares. As the prophet Isaiah tells us in this week's theme verse, He's watching and ready to lift us up when we grow tired and weary. So are the loved ones who have gone ahead of us to heaven. They are cheering us on as they would if they were on earth with us.

But most of all we need to focus on the love of the Lord, who promises to strengthen us, and live out of a grateful heart.

$\mathcal{P}$RAYER FOR THIS WEEK
*Father God, thank You for creating us*
*in Your image and giving us strength*
*to always reach our full potential.*
*Help us learn to do our best out of love for You!*
*In Jesus's name, amen.*

# THE WRITING ON THE WALL

*Suddenly the fingers of a human hand*
*appeared and wrote on the plaster of the wall,*
*near the lampstand in the royal palace.*
*The king watched the hand as it wrote.*

DANIEL 5:5

Don't you love to watch kids draw and color with crayons, markers, pencils, paints, eyeliner? I do too, until it's on the walls, doors, cabinets, counters, or anything that looks like a blank canvas to them. Our youngest daughter, Jordan, decided to use the counter in the bathroom as her blank canvas. She was being quiet, which is never a good sign, so I went to check on her. As I walked past the bathroom, I saw my makeup bag out and my eyeliners were all over the floor. As I stepped in to pick them up, I saw eyeliner scribbles all over the counter!

"Jordan Elizabeth! Come in here!" I called. She came running out of her room and I was standing in the doorway of the bathroom. She stopped in her tracks and, as innocently as she could, said, "Yes, Mommy?" I said, "Did you write on the counter with my eyeliner?" "No, Mommy, it wasn't me." It was only her and I home at the time and it wasn't there after her sisters went to school so . . . she was busted. I said, "Well, if you didn't do it, who did?" She replied, "Um, I don't know?" As I went to the kitchen to get some cleaner, I heard her say she found who did it! I walked into the living room, and she was standing by our cat, who was laying on the floor with an eyeliner pencil next to him. She exclaimed, "He did it, Mommy!" Y'all, I could hardly keep my composure. I said, "He did, did he?" "Yep, he sure did!" and off she went. I was just glad it was the counter and not the wall.

King Belshazzar was drinking and having a good time when he decided to order the gold and silver goblets that his father, Nebuchadnezzar, had taken from the temple in Jerusalem. Here's how Daniel tells the story in Daniel 5:3-6:

So they brought in the gold goblets that had been taken from the temple of God in Jerusalem, and the king and his nobles, his wives and his concubines drank from them. As they drank the wine, they praised the gods of gold and silver, of bronze, wood and stone. Suddenly the fingers of a human hand appeared and wrote on the plaster of the wall, near the lampstand in the royal palace. The king watched the hand as it wrote. His face turned pale, and he was so frightened that his legs became weak, and his knees were knocking.

This is where the saying, "Can't you see the writing on the wall?" comes from. Can you imagine being at the table with Belshazzar and witnessing it? I'm going to go out on limb here and say that I bet he wasn't the only one with a pale face and knocking knees. He didn't humble himself before God, nor had his father, Nebuchadnezzar, for a time. They became arrogant and wouldn't acknowledge that the Most High God is sovereign over all kingdoms on earth and sets over them anyone he wishes.

It's a dangerous thing to go against God Almighty and fall into His hands with an arrogant heart, dishonoring God and His temple. But still, knowing what his father had done, Belshazzar deliberately did the same thing. Whereas Nebuchadnezzar returned to God humbled, Belshazzar lost his life. Pride is one of the seven deadly sins, and it goes before a fall. It went before Belshazzar. I never want to be so prideful or arrogant that I forget God is first above everything and in all things!

*P*RAYER FOR THIS WEEK
*Father God, renew our hearts to be humble*
*and full of thanksgiving as we come before You.*
*In Jesus's name, amen.*

# NONFICTION

*You saw with your own eyes the great trials, the signs
and wonders, the mighty hand and outstretched arm,
with which the L*ORD *your God brought you out.
The L*ORD *your God will do the same to all the peoples
you now fear. Moreover, the L*ORD *your God will send
the hornet among them until even the survivors who
hide from you have perished. Do not be terrified
by them, for the L*ORD *your God who is among you is
a great and awesome God. . . . But the L*ORD *your God
will deliver them over to you, throwing them into
great confusion until they are destroyed.*

DEUTERONOMY 7:19–21, 23

When Fredrick the Great asked his trusted advisor for the single stron-
gest piece of evidence that proved the existence of God, the advisor answered him: "The Jews, sir, the Jews."

As I shared earlier, I have a love and passion for our Jewish brothers and sisters, their culture and traditions, the Jewish religion, how the
Jewish people are "the apple of God's eye" and understanding what that
means. We would not have the Messiah, Jesus Christ, without the Jewish
lineage. I do not understand the hatred of Jewish people by groups that
say they are Christian and believe in God and His Son Jesus but hate Jews.
Hello . . . Jesus is Jewish!

There are people today in the twenty-first century that spew the
same anti-Semitic vitriol reminiscent of Haman, Hitler, Stalin, and Mussolini to name a few. Some tried to annihilate the Jewish people. "The
Final Solution to the Jewish Question" was Hitler's main plan to rid the
world of the Jews by extermination. It involved murdering and torturing

innocent men, women, and children because of his hatred of the Jews—the Holocaust.

He blamed them for his lot in life as an adult and he started to devise his plot against the Jews in his book *Mein Kampf* (*My Struggle*). Hitler said, "The best way to take control over a people and control them utterly is to take a little of their freedom at a time, to erode rights by a thousand tiny and almost imperceptible reductions. In this way the people will not see those rights and freedoms being removed until past the point at which these changes cannot be reversed." How horrifyingly evil Hitler was then and his ideologies are still today!

From 1941 to 1945 much of the European Jewry were sent to concentration camps. If you were deemed fit to work, you lived to work yourself to death in the camps or as slave labor for German companies such as I. G. Farben and Bayer. Children were used for medical experiments at the hands of camp doctors like Josef Mengele. Jews were not human to the Nazis. Older adults, small children, the sick, and the handicapped were deemed unfit to live and they were sent to the gas chambers and poisoned with Zyclon B gas, then burned in the crematoriums. There were so many murdered in the gas chambers that the crematorium could not keep up and they began piling the bodies in the camp. By the time word got to the Nazi camp leaders that the Allies were coming, they tried to destroy as much evidence as they could. They began tearing down the crematoriums, taking what prisoners were left on death marches until they died or were shot if they could not keep up.

On January 27, 1945, the Russian Army liberated Auschwitz. When the camps were liberated, General Dwight D. Eisenhower predicted that one day people would deny the Holocaust , deny that it even happened. He then ordered as many pictures as possible to be taken and to have the Germans from the surrounding towns and villages be brought inside the camps to see the atrocities that happened there to prevent the events from being labeled as "propaganda."

There are Holocaust deniers that say it never happened, that it is fake, it is a lie, it is a hoax.

It. Did. Happen. More than six million Jewish men, women, and children were murdered. Fact.

Ironically, Hitler made you prove your ethnicity through the Nuremburg Race Laws, but he could not prove his own. It is rumored that there was some Jewish blood in his family tree.

God told His chosen people, the Jews, that they are "the apple of his eye" and that He who protects Israel will neither "slumber nor sleep" (Deuteronomy 32:10; Psalm 121:4).

*True story!* Hitler failed in annihilating the Jews! . . .

$\mathcal{P}$RAYER FOR THIS WEEK

*Father, help us to never ever forget*
*the Holocaust and that You are the great and*
*mighty God who will protect us as well!*
*In Jesus's name, amen.*

# ARE THE BEST THINGS IN LIFE FREE?

*You were bought with the precious blood of Christ's death.*
*He was a pure and perfect sacrificial Lamb.*
1 PETER 1:19

How many times when you were a kid did your mom or dad say, "We are not cooling or heating the outside?" My parents said it too, but my favorite saying Dad said was, "Close the door! You're letting out the bought air!" I would say, "Nuh-uh, Dad, air is free!" as I would roll my eyes and laugh. My dad always responded, "Are you paying for it?" "Um, no." "Well, when you are paying for it, you can prop the door open. Until then, *close the door!*"

Fast-forward forty years . . . guess what? I have turned into my dad! He would be so proud! LOL. I have said the same thing to our kids, grandkids, and even the dog. I didn't think it was such a big deal until I was paying for it. Now it is a whole new ballgame. I started taking notice when it was coming out of my pocket. Isn't it funny how, when someone else is paying for things, we don't worry about the cost as much? But when it's our turn to pay, then it hurts.

Someone else "picked up the tab" for us, too, at a higher cost than we could ever pay back. It cost Jesus His life. Jesus shed His blood for us so we would never have to. Read this week's verses again from 1 Peter 1:19. Jesus loved us so much to die for our sins, so we would never be separated from Him. All we must do is pray and believe that Jesus is the Christ, the Son of Living God, and accept Him as our Lord and Savior who died on the cross to save us from our sin.

We flippantly say, "I would die for him (or her or this or that)," but would we? Would we have the courage to do so without hesitation, as Jesus did for us on the cross? Afterward He asked His Father to forgive us for nailing Him to the cross. We had no idea it was for our sin.

He loved us so much that He bought us with His precious blood, so we can be with Him in eternity. Nothing is free. Not freedom. Not life. Not salvation.

### $\mathcal{P}$RAYER FOR THIS WEEK
*Jesus, thank You for loving me so much that*
*You paid my ransom with Your blood without*
*hesitation. Help us to never forget the cost.*
*In Your precious name, Jesus, amen.*

# WORRY ENDS
# WHERE FAITH BEGINS

*Can any one of you by worrying add a single hour to your life?*
MATTHEW 6:27

August 8, 2013, was the day that changed my life and my perspective as I knew it. In the days leading up to that day, I had a feeling that something was physically wrong and decided to go to the doctor. I felt like I might be having a pancreatitis attack, having had them in the past. When I went to the doctor, I insisted on a CT scan, as I had a fear of pancreatic cancer or cancer of some type. My doctor relented and sent me for a CT scan to calm my fear more than anything.

He ordered it stat and after it was finished, I was told it was nothing emergent and to follow up with my doctor for the results. I assumed everything was okay. I called my doctor the next day to go over my results, but he was off, so I left a message. The next day was August 8, and my phone rang before nine in the morning. I saw it was the doctor's office; they were calling to tell me my doctor wanted to see me, to go over my results. My heart sank. I got up and went to work but was very distracted because I knew it was something bad.

As I drove past a church I saw every day in our neighborhood, God turned my head to look at the sign. It read, "Worry ends where faith begins." I knew God was speaking to me. I came home from work and told my husband we had to go in for the results. He knew something was wrong too. So we went in and waited for what seemed like an eternity. My doctor finally came in with the results—kidney cancer. It felt like all the oxygen in the room had been sucked out. I looked over at my husband, his head dropped, and my heart broke. We went to see a urologist who told us it was stage one. *Praise God!* It also looked like the cancer was in the middle of my kidney, which more than likely meant I would lose the whole kidney. Fine. "How fast can we do this?" I asked. His nurse said that he was booked out three weeks. I am not going to lie, I freaked out a little bit. "You are going to leave this cancer in me for three weeks?!" Little did I know it was part of God's plan.

Surgery was scheduled for August 27. An eternity, or it might as well have been. It turned out to be such a blessing, because in those three weeks, God moved in me, for me, and with me. I truly experienced that peace that passes *all* understanding. Let me just tell you, it is a beautiful place to be! During that time, we told our kids, and the rest of our family. It was heartbreaking to see the fear in their eyes of what could happen. In those moments, God gave me supernatural strength and peace to keep it together for everyone else, while my God and Savior was keeping me together. I knew how I handled this was going to dictate how everyone around me would handle it.

Reread Matthew 6:27, our theme verse for the week. How much time do we waste worrying about stuff? *Too much!* Worry is a form of fear. God tells us in His Word 365 times to "fear not." Hmmm, one verse a day for a year. I would say He really doesn't want us to worry or fear anything. God is *bigger* than any worry or fear we have!

Long story short, I had surgery to remove my kidney. My margins were clear, totally stage one. No chemo or radiation! *He is greater* than our fears!

No God; no peace. Know God; know peace.

### ℘RAYER FOR THIS WEEK

*Jesus, give us the peace that only You can give, and the blessed assurance that You will never leave us nor forsake us.*
*In Your precious name, amen.*

## What Cancer Cannot Do

It cannot cripple love.
It cannot shatter hope.
It cannot kill friendship.
It cannot erode the spirit.
It cannot take away faith.
It cannot silence courage.
It cannot destroy peace.
It cannot suppress memories.
It cannot conquer the soul.
It cannot steal eternal life.

ROBERT L. LYNN

# JUST NINE MORE MINUTES

*Come to me,*
*all you who are weary and burdened,*
*and I will give you rest*
MATTHEW 11:28

Hi, my name is Sue, and I'm a serial snoozer. I will usually set my alarm for thirty minutes before I want to get up, well, twenty-seven minutes to be exact. Have you ever wondered why the snooze is set for nine minutes and not ten? There is a theory and science behind it, believe it or not. Alarm clocks added a snooze button in 1956. General Electric's Telechron Snooz-Alarm, and the snooze lasted . . . you guessed it, nine minutes.

Before the snooze button was added, alarm clocks had a standard gear setup already. The creators were having a hard time lining the gears up for a ten-minute snooze. It wasn't possible, and a double-digit snooze was going to be harder to program. They opted for the single-digit snooze, and the designers decided to go with the less complicated design. Hence the nine-minute snooze. Nine minutes is apparently more beneficial because it's a long enough time for a brief rest. If you go to the ten-minute mark, you start to fall back into a deep sleep, and it's not good for your internal clock either. Okay I'm tired now.

My husband used to say, "Why don't you just get up at the time you want to get up?" (My snoozing bothered him.) I said, "No, because then I can't hit the snooze." Many years later . . . Hi, this is my husband, Dale, and he's a serial snoozer too!

We do these silly things like hitting the snooze for a few more moments of rest, but is it really rest? Restorative, renewing, peaceful rest? No. There's only one place to go when we are weary, tired, and burdened with life and everyday stress—Jesus.

Jesus said in Matthew 11:28, "Come to me, all you who are weary and burdened, and I will give you rest." Not just *a few* of you come. Not *some* of you come. Jesus said *all* of you. That's you. That's me. There is nothing like resting in His righteousness and giving Jesus all our burdens. We are weak, but He is strong. Yes, Jesus loves me, the Bible tells me so!

### $\mathcal{P}$RAYER FOR THIS WEEK

*Jesus, help us to remember that You are*
*the only one we can go to for true rest. Thank You*
*for always standing beside us ready to take*
*the weight of our burdens so we can rest.*
*In Jesus's name, amen.*

# GROUNDED

*Children, obey your parents in everything,*
*for this pleases the Lord.*
COLOSSIANS 3:20

How many times have you been grounded? If you have kids, how many times have you grounded them? We got in trouble a lot growing up, whether it was not being where we said we were going, coming home past curfew, or hiding report cards. When you don't do what you're told, you get grounded.

We always say, "I'm going to parent *my* kids differently." We'll let them stay out all night, they don't have to call and check in, and as long as they pass with at least all Ds on report cards, it's all good! We think we can just allow them to have no rules, but then it happens! You open your mouth, and your mom or dad comes flying out of it! How the tables turn when you become the parent. You realize that you have become worse than your parents. I totally understand now, it all makes sense. It's about protecting our most precious possessions with rules and boundaries that are nonnegotiable.

In Colossians 3:20 we are told, "Children, obey your parents in everything, for this pleases the Lord." Guess who the children are? Us. His Word gives us our rules and boundaries, and we are expected to follow them. Guess who the parent is? God. He's the parent loving us when we mess up or make bad choices that hurt us. He is waiting for us to repent, and He forgives us every single time, just as we do with our own children. When we realize the rules are there because we are loved so much that our Father wants to protect us, we will respect the rules even more.

Rules + Discipline = LOVE

### PRAYER FOR THIS WEEK

*Father God, help us see all the boundaries*
*and guidance that you give us*
*as coming out of Your wise and protective love!*
*Thank You for Your words and instructions*
*from the only rule book that matters—the Bible.*
*In Jesus's name, amen.*

# IT'S A WONDERFUL LIFE

*She will give birth to a son,*
*and you are to give him the name Jesus,*
*because he will save his people from their sins.*
MATTHEW 1:21

Christmas. Shopping. Cooking. Wrapping. Decorating. Family. And Clarence. Do you feel tired already? Overwhelmed? We all get that way at some point during the holidays. There are certain things even at my age that bring back wonderful memories of Christmas—snow, peppermint, hot chocolate, popcorn balls, *How the Grinch Stole Christmas, White Christmas, Rudolph the Red-Nosed Reindeer,* and my most favorite of all, *A Charlie Brown Christmas.* I must hear Linus tell the Christmas Story of Jesus's birth. "Lights please" . . . with a lisp.

As I got older, I discovered *It's a Wonderful Life* and it has become a staple movie any time of the year, with George Bailey and his new/old buddy Clarence Odbody, AS2 (Angel Second Class). Clarence is on a mission from God to convince George to not commit suicide and to understand just how important he was. Without George, Bedford Falls would become a grim and unhappy place—Pottersville. If his mission is successful, Clarence will get his wings! AS1 (Angel First Class).

George Bailey decides he wants to live, thanks to Clarence, and what he tells George still gives me goosebumps every time. "One man's life touches so many others." *Truth!* Attaboy Clarence! ("Zuzu Bailey: "Look, Daddy. Teacher says every time a bell rings an angel gets his wings.") That's right.

In Matthew 1:21 we read, "She will give birth to a son, and you are to give him the name Jesus, because he will save his people from their sins." This one man's life has touched so many others. Jesus's life and death has touched all those who believe in Him. Imagine what this world would look like without the promise of eternal life through repentance and the salvation that only *He* can give. We have the promise of a wonderful life with Him!

### $\mathcal{P}$RAYER FOR THIS WEEK

*Jesus, thank You for the wonderful life You*
*have given us through Your life, death, and*
*resurrection. Help us see how You want to use*
*our lives to touch those around us as well.*
*In Jesus's name, amen.*

# SHOAH

*That day will be a day of wrath—*
*a day of distress and anguish,*
*a day of trouble and ruin,*
*a day of darkness and gloom,*
*a day of clouds and blackness.*

ZEPHANIAH 1:15

Our theme verse this week is about the great day of the Lord, the future day when God's judgment will be pronounced. *Shoah* in Hebrew and signifies total and utter destruction. Similarly, "Holocaust" comes from the Greek *holos* and *kaustos* and when they are put together it means "totally burnt," which is exactly what happened to the Jews during WWII in Europe. More than six million Jews were murdered by death squads called Einsatzgruppen. They were taken to the gas chambers, and their poor bodies were burned to ashes.

If we held one minute of silence for every victim of the Holocaust . . . we would be silent for eleven and a half years. Sobering, isn't it? One million of those deaths were children, most of whom were deemed unfit to live. If you were twins you were "spared" for ghastly medical experimentations until death. It was unfathomable then, as it is still today.

January 27, 1945, was the day that the Russian Army liberated Auschwitz-Birkenau, and it is International Holocaust Remembrance Day. Regardless of your religion or ethnicity you need to remember the victims of the Holocaust. This day also acknowledges all other forms of Nazi persecution and other genocides that have taken place.

*Never forget. Never forget. Never forget. Never forget. If we do forget, we are doomed to repeat history.*

### 𝒫RAYER FOR THIS WEEK

*Father God, never let us forget the Shoah*
*that your people have faced throughout the years.*
*But also, never let us forget that*
*the great day of the LORD is yet to come.*
*In Jesus's name, amen.*

# DON'T MAKE ME . . .

*Live self-controlled, upright and godly lives in this present age,*
*while we wait for the blessed hope—the appearing of the glory*
*of our great God and Savior, Jesus Christ, who gave himself for*
*us to redeem us from all wickedness and to purify for himself*
*a people that are his very own, eager to do what is good.*

TITUS 2:12-14

"Don't make me come in there!" "Don't make me turn this car around!"
"Don't make me take that from you both!" "Don't make me tell you again!"
Sound familiar? If I had a nickel for every time I heard that or said that . . .
I would be rich! My mom and dad had a little sign that hung in the dining
room that said, "Don't make me come down there . . . God."

Do you think that God talks to us like that? We dreaded hearing that
from our parents, because we knew we would be in trouble if they had
to come intervene. But when Jesus did come down to earth to intervene,
what was he saying to us? As our Bible verse says, He came to give Himself
and to redeem us, not to condemn us. And the next time He comes back
down here, it will be to take us with Him to paradise!

We should turn our eyes to heaven with great anticipation and
readiness for our triumphant Savior and King, Jesus Christ, to come for
us, His church. Hallelujah to the Lamb of God! Come, Lord Jesus, Come!

### *P*RAYER FOR THIS WEEK
*Jesus, help us to live self-controlled*
*and godly lives, always ready for your return,*
*but not out of fear of Your condemnation,*
*but out of love for You, our Redeemer.*
*In Your name, amen.*

# HOW OLD AM I . . . REALLY?

*Gray hair is a crown of splendor;*
*it is attained in the way of righteousness.*
PROVERBS 16:31

Is age just a number or a state of mind? Do we age like fine wine and cheese and get better with age? I think so. I remember when I was quite young hearing my mom say she was thirty-three. I thought wow. She. Is. Old. She's got to be as old as the Crypt Keeper, you know, from the show. I couldn't imagine being that old, until I was. Not old, just that age.

That's when it happened, one of our kids asked how old I was. I said, "In my thirties." Out of the mouths of babes came, "Dang Mom, you are old." I said, "I am not old!" Or am I? I noticed gray hairs, a wrinkle when I smiled (which then turned to three), and soon my forehead looked like someone skied across it. Okay, I'm not going down without a fight!

My hands were getting wrinkles, what the heck happened? My mom had beautiful hands and beautiful nails. I always wanted my hands to look like hers. Even as she aged, I thought she still had beautiful hands. My mom passed away in 2019. I looked down at my own hands and realized I do have my mother's hands even though they are aging. But aging has a beauty all its own. I do have wrinkles and gray hair; I don't mind it at all.

As our proverb for this week says, "Gray hair is a CROWN OF SPLENDOR." Talk about growing old gracefully! A crown of splendor? I'll take it! He created you, me, and everyone else with what we tend to see as flaws as we age. He created those beautiful additions for a reason, and we should wear them proudly.

*P*RAYER FOR THIS WEEK
*Father, help us not to look at ourselves*
*through flawed worldly eyes,*
*help us to see ourselves as*
*the beautiful person You created.*
*In Jesus's name, amen.*

# SOUL SONG

*My heart, O God, is steadfast;*
*I will sing and make music with all my soul.*
PSALM 108:1

Do you have a favorite song that you just love to belt out in the car, the shower, cleaning the house, at work, or anywhere you are comfortable? I do not sing in the shower, but I will in the car and when I am home alone. Operative word A-L-O-N-E. When I sing with the radio or my playlist, I must say that I do sound exactly like Celine Dion, Whitney Houston, and Adele all rolled into one. I have been waiting for a big fat recording contract. Can you believe I do not have one yet? Well, I can, because they are who I want to sound like. Instead, dogs were howling, that is how bad I sounded.

I love to sing, but the only one that loves to hear me sing is God. On Sunday mornings at church, I love to sing praises and worship to the God of heaven and earth. Is there a song that overwhelms you with emotion to sing? It moves you to tears so that you cannot audibly be heard? That's when your soul takes over singing, praising, and worshiping God.

"My heart, O God, is steadfast; I will sing and make music with all my soul" (Psalm 108:1). David shows us the only type of praise and worship God wants—worship that is from our very souls. I have a picture in my living room that says, "Then sings my soul" and every time I read those words, "My Savior God to thee, how great Thou art" follows. Let your heart and soul sing out to your Savior, *How great Thou art!*

*P*RAYER FOR THIS WEEK
*O Lord our God, how great You are!*
*Thank You for welcoming my worship,*
*no matter what it sounds like. Help me to bring*
*my whole soul to You in worship.*
*In Jesus's name, amen.*

# ANNELIES MARIE FRANK

BORN JUNE 12, 1929—DIED FEBRUARY/MARCH 1945

"Anne Frank" is how she has become known to millions of readers and writers young and old. I'm sure most of us have read her very famous diary as a required reading in school. I felt like I was a fly on the wall in their tiny living quarters. She was truly gifted from God with her ability to write her thoughts, feelings, emotions, and dreams so eloquently at just thirteen years old. She shared so much with "Kitty" the name for her diary and closest confidante. And thanks to Miep Gies, one of the Frank's close friends and supporters while they were in hiding, Anne's diary was found and kept in hopes of giving it to Anne after the war. Sadly, Anne died just weeks before Bergen-Belsen Concentration Camp was liberated. Miep returned it to Otto Frank her father. After reading it Otto ultimately wanted to share it, it was first published in Germany and France in 1950. Then it was published in the United States in 1952. Her wisdom as a thirteen-year-old Jewish girl in hiding from the Nazis is sweet, unabashed, innocent, hopeful, and thought-provoking beyond her years.

Here are some quotes from her diary. You be the judge.

"Whoever is happy will make others happy."

"In spite of everything, I still believe that people are really good at heart."

"I don't think of all the misery, but the beauty that still remains."

"Memories mean more to me than dresses."

"In the long run, the sharpest weapon of all is a kind and gentle spirit."

"No one has ever become poor by giving."

"I can shake off everything as I write; my sorrows disappear, my courage reborn."

"Dead people receive more flowers than the living ones because regret is stronger than gratitude."

"Look at how a single candle can both defy and define the darkness."

"Laziness may appear attractive, but work gives satisfaction."

"People can tell you to keep your mouth shut, but that doesn't stop you from having your own opinion."

*Wow!* It's hard to keep this kind of positive outlook, especially as a thirteen-year-old in the middle of a dire situation. Let her words challenge you today, as you consider your own outlook on life and the trials you face.

*P*RAYER FOR THIS WEEK

*Father, thank You for promising to give us*
*wisdom and courage. Help us to humbly submit*
*our outlook on life to You, finding the "beauty*
*that still remains" in Your master plan.*
*In Jesus's name, amen.*

# SHALOM

*The Lord bless you*
*and keep you;*
*the Lord make his face shine on you*
*and be gracious to you;*
*the Lord turn his face toward you*
*and give you peace.*
NUMBERS 6:24–26

*Shalom* (shah-LOME) is the Hebrew word for peace or well-being. It is also used for hello and good-bye. Rabbi Robert I. Kahn of Houston, Texas, encapsulates the difference between the ancient Roman word for "peace" and the ancient Hebrew *shalom*:

> One can dictate a peace; shalom is a mutual agreement.
> Peace is a temporary pact; shalom is a permanent agreement.
> One can make a peace treaty; shalom is the condition of peace.
> Peace can be negative, the absence of commotion.
> Shalom is positive, the presence of serenity.
> Peace can be partial; shalom is whole.
> Peace can be piecemeal; shalom is complete.

> True peace, *shalom*, rests with God.
> Know God; know peace. That peace is the peace that passes all understanding. This kind of peace melts away your anxiety and fear, as He leads you beside the still waters. This kind of peace melts away the

uncertainty that creeps in and makes your mind race, as He leads your mind beside the still waters. This kind of peace stays with you, even as your heart is broken in a million pieces, as He leads you beside the still waters and picks up the broken pieces of your heart and carries them while He also carries you.

This kind of peace comforts you when you get a life-changing diagnosis, as He leads you beside the still waters and tells you, "I am the Great Physician." This kind of peace melts away the anger and hurt, that makes you want to hurt back, as He leads you beside the still waters and reminds you that vengeance is His to repay. This kind of peace melts away the lies you tell yourself when you feel ugly, unloved, and unworthy, while He leads you beside the still waters and tells you, you are His perfect, beautiful creation and His love for you is unconditional and unfathomable.

The Lord bless you and keep you. The Lord make His face shine upon you and be gracious to you. The Lord lift up His countenance on you and give you shalom. (Numbers 6:24–26 CJB)

*Shalom. Shalom. Shalom.*

### $\mathcal{P}$RAYER FOR THIS WEEK
*Father God, You are our peace, our shalom.*
*May Your Holy Spirit guard our hearts*
*and minds so that we will know Your peace*
*that passes all understanding.*
*In Jesus name, amen.*

# OVERCOMER

*You, dear children, are from God and have*
*overcome them, because the one who is in you*
*is greater than the one who is in the world*
1 JOHN 4:4

On the 8th of August, 2013, as I shared previously, I was diagnosed with kidney cancer. My surgery, however, was not scheduled until August 27. It was the longest three weeks of my life. No matter how hard I tried to keep my mind from dwelling on the worst-case scenarios, Satan would whisper to my fears. I know he is a liar. He was trying to scare me, and honestly, on one particular day, he was winning. My grandmother used to say, "If you give the devil an inch, he will take a foot and if you give him a foot, he will drive." She also said, "If you write on one of your shoes the name "Satan" and on the other shoe "Go back to hell," then you walk on him all day. And if you are walking on him, he stays where he belongs—below." I love my grandma.

So while I was driving and crying, and Satan was trying to take the wheel of my mind, a song came on the radio that I had heard a million times—"Hold Me Jesus" by Big Daddy Weave. This time it caught me by the ears of my heart. Right after that song came "Overcomer" by Mandisa. Satan *ran*! God spoke *shalom* to me in those two songs.

I had so much peace. Just as we read in 1 John 4:4, I was reminded that my God is bigger, stronger, higher than any other or anything. And I am an overcomer! I knew going into surgery that God was going before me and that He will always be by my side. He carries me and He will carry you.

### Prayer for this week

*Hold me, Jesus, cause I'm shaking like a leaf.*
*You have been King of my glory,*
*won't you be my Prince of Peace.*
*In Jesus's name, amen.*

# PAVEMENT

*The twelve gates were twelve pearls,*
*each gate made of a single pearl.*
*The great street of the city was of gold,*
*as pure as transparent glass.*

REVELATION 21:21

My husband, Dale, has been in law enforcement for over thirty years, and in that time, he has worked with a lot of different partners on different beats. As with any place of work, you can have good and bad coworkers, some you like to be around more than others. He had a small group that he considered friends. About ten years ago, one such partner and friend, told Dale that he and his wife had started buying gold as an investment. When things start "happening," he said, it's the only currency for trade that will be worth anything.

So after they had this conversation a time or two my husband said, "Why would I invest in gold here, when it's the pavement in heaven?

Streets of gold are what we will be walking on." Dale would use things like that to witness to him. Sadly, he lost his battle with cancer in the spring of 2022. But now he is walking on streets gold! Though gold holds some value for us here and now, our ultimate treasure is in heaven.

Try to envision those streets of gold that John told about in this week's verse. Wow . . . can you imagine the magnitude of that city? What beauty awaits us in heaven with Jesus, we can only imagine. One day very soon the King is coming! Hallelujah to the Lamb!

### $\mathcal{P}$RAYER FOR THIS WEEK

*Loving Father, thank You for the beauty*
*of Your creation on earth and in heaven*
*and for Your precious Son Jesus.*
*Help us to value what You value*
*as we wait for You to come again.*
*In Jesus's name, amen.*

# A STITCH IN TIME

*Many are the plans in a person's heart,*
*but it is the LORD's purpose that prevails.*

PROVERBS 19:21

Do you remember the old, crocheted Afghan's that were frequently laid across the backs of couches? They might have zigzag designs, multicolored squares, straight stripes, or scalloped designs. I would be willing to bet that someone in your family has probably made a few of those blankets. Whether as a Christmas present, a birthday present, a wedding present, or for a baby shower, those blankets were the best kind of gift you could get. Someone took the time to hand make a beautiful piece of art just for you. A labor of love.

My great-grandmother made one such blanket, a bedspread, that is about forty-seven years old now. I remember watching her start it and thinking this will take a hundred years, because she didn't use thick yarn—she used thin crochet thread! She used a popcorn stitch pattern, that was very pretty. After what seemed like an eternity, it was finished, and it was beautiful. I ran my fingers over each popcorn cluster. It was amazing on the top side. The back side was flat and plain compared to the top. It was harder to see a design on the back.

That can be how it feels when we do not understand God's plan for things in our lives. Reread our verse for this week. Are you focused on your own plans or the Lord's purposes?

Just like the stitches on the blanket, God knows the pattern He has set for our lives. He sees the beautiful design of every single stitch, where and how it goes. We see the back side with the stray stitch here or there, the plain side without a definitive pattern. But we can rest assured that God is always in control. When we get to heaven, everything will make sense and we will see the beauty of His design for our life. We often think we know better, but He always knows best.

*P*RAYER FOR THIS WEEK
*Father God, thank You*
*for Your beautiful design that is my life*
*and for being in control of every detail.*
*Help me to trust that You are working all things*
*together for Your good purposes.*
*In Jesus's name, amen.*

# ABBA

*"Abba, Father," he said,*
*"everything is possible for you.*
*Take this cup from me. Yet not what I will,*
*but what you will."*

MARK 14:36

Have you ever heard someone call out to *Abba*? No, I'm not talking about the band from the seventies with the same name. *Abba* is Hebrew for "Father, I will obey you." (HIM PUBLICATIONS) Have we always obeyed our parents? Most of us at some point in our lives have not. Whether it was something small like not staying out of the cookie jar before dinner or something big like taking your first underage drink of alcohol. When we test the waters of disobedience and get in trouble, what is the first thing that happens? Remorse sets in and we feel terrible, because we let our parents down. I always felt worse because I knew better, but I did it anyway. And on an occasion when it was a monumental screwup, who did we want to come and save the day? Dad. He could make you feel safe. Even though he was disappointed, he still loved you, despite the fact that you did not obey his rules.

Jesus is the only one I know that fully obeyed *everything* His Father instructed, even in the garden the night Jesus was arrested. Jesus did something we as flawed human beings could never do! He agreed to take our sins upon Himself and be nail to the cross.

Listen again to His prayer in the garden. Jesus went to *Abba*, His Father, was human on our behalf, yet willing to obey His Father by going to the cross, not for anything He did but for everything we did.

### $\mathcal{P}$RAYER FOR THIS WEEK

*Jesus, thank You for loving me so much*
*You took my sin and ransomed me with Your blood*
*through Your death and resurrection.*
*Help me to come willingly and obediently*
*to my Abba Father, just like You did.*
*In Your name, amen.*

# I NEED A NEW JOB OR A NEW ATTITUDE

*Whatever you do, work at it with all your heart,*
*as working for the Lord, not for human masters,*
*since you know that you will receive*
*an inheritance from the Lord as a reward.*
*It is the Lord Christ you are serving.*
COLOSSIANS 3:23-24

I have had more jobs that I didn't like than jobs that I did. You can probably relate. There is an old saying that says, "If you love what you do, you
will never work a day in your life." I must be honest here, I often start
out loving a new job. But inevitably something or someone happens to
change my mind. We have all had situations beyond our control at work,
where management and their way of doing things seems wrong. They are
not in the trenches with us, but yet the decisions they make affect *us* not
them. "I hate my job" happens. I'd go on to another job and I love it until

. . . maybe there are some people I do not like. I am not sticking around! Time to go.

Looking at our verses for this week, I could see that the problem was me and my attitude. That stung.

Well, if that doesn't put it into perspective, I am not sure what will. I am working for the Lord and no one else. I don't have to worry about what I think management should or should not do. I work for the Lord. I don't have to worry about not liking someone. I am working for the Lord. The Lord will reward. There are always going to be people, management, and situations that I don't like or agree with and that is okay because I am working for the Lord. He is my boss, and He needs me to keep my eyes on Him and He will take care of the rest. He has the best bonuses and benefits!

### $\mathcal{P}$RAYER FOR THIS WEEK

*Lord, thank You for always taking care of me.*
*Help me remember that everything I need is in You*
*and that all my work is done for You.*
*In Jesus's name, amen.*

# WE NEED A REVIVAL

*Restore us, L*ORD *God Almighty;*
*make your face shine on us,*
*that we may be saved.*

PSALM 80:19

*Will you not revive us again,*
*that your people may rejoice in you?*

PSALM 85:6

Do you remember when churches would have revivals? Sometimes they would last days or weeks at a time. I loved going to them. We would have guest preachers and a lot of times we wouldn't get out until nine or nine thirty at night. One year we had David Ring come and lead our revival, what an amazing gift it was. If you are not familiar with him, he was born dead for eighteen minutes and developed cerebral palsy. He speaks with an impediment and has some mobility issues but none of that stops him.

He will tell you "I have cerebral palsy. What's your problem?" God has blessed him and his ministry.

It is about getting back to the basics of life. We need to put God first. We need to put God back into our schools. We need to stop worrying about being politically correct. Instead, we need to concern ourselves with doing what is right according to God's Word. And we cannot do it without God! We need a revival in our churches, in our government, in our country, in our world, in our lives.

When we make God the focus and return to Him, He will restore and revive our hearts, our churches, our country, and our world. We need some good ol' tent revivals like Billy Graham did years ago that would go on for weeks, that will set you and your faith on fire again! Can I get a witness?!?!

## *P*RAYER FOR THIS WEEK

*Father God, send a revival to restore our world*
*and Your Holy Fire to restore our hearts.*
*In Jesus's name, amen.*

# IN THE GARDEN

*When Jesus' followers saw what*
*was going to happen, they said,*
*"Lord, should we strike with our swords?"*
*And one of them struck the servant*
*of the high priest, cutting off his right ear.*
*But Jesus answered, "No more of this!"*
*And he touched the man's ear and healed him.*

LUKE 22:49-51

There is one person that is mentioned in Scripture that I think would have had an incredible story to tell and his name is Malchus. He is the servant of Caiaphas the high priest, and he was with the group that Judas Iscariot brought into the garden to arrest Jesus. I wonder if he was a loyal servant or was it just a job? Did he grumble about being out late? Do you think he had an opinion about Jesus or why the religious leaders wanted him arrested?

I think he was someone who did as he was told, and that night was no different for him, until he walked into the garden with Judas. The moment Jesus was betrayed, chaos ensued as Peter drew his sword and cut off Malchus's ear. I imagine him dropping to his knees as he is holding the side of his head, blood running down his face and hand. And then it happens—he is kneeling before the Son of God, who heals and restores his ear! Can you imagine?! If he did not have an opinion about Jesus before, he does now. I would like to think he walked up to Caiaphas, told him what happened, and said, "I quit." Maybe he rushed out to find Jesus or the disciples and asked how to become a follower of the Way.

Maybe Malchus will be waiting in heaven to tell his amazing story of transformation.

### $\mathcal{P}$RAYER FOR THIS WEEK

*Jesus, thank You for being the Way and*
*showing us the Way in all circumstances.*
*In Your name, amen.*

# WHAT IS LOVE?

*For God so loved the world that he gave*
*his one and only Son, that whoever believes in him*
*shall not perish but have eternal life.*
*For God did not send his Son into the world to condemn*
*the world, but to save the world through him.*

JOHN 3:16–17

Good question and a million different answers. Some of the best answers come from kids. When the interviewer from the Jubilee Project asked, "What is love?" here are a few of the responses: "Loving someone is, like, a lot of eye contact." "It makes me feel warm and cozy like a pillow." "It feels like you'll never be lonely." "True love is a mixture of friendship, appreciation, and like, happiness." "If my mom wants to read a book in bed my dad will go to bed. But if my mom wants to watch TV my dad will watch TV." There you have it, Love in its simplest definitions out of the mouths of babes. So, what is it to you?

Love is something different to all of us—taking out the garbage, cooking dinner and cleaning up afterward, flowers just because, folding the laundry, putting down the cell phone and being present with each other, working hard to provide for your family, and the list goes on.

Reread through our theme verse again. That, my friend, is the true definition of what love is. God's Word and His Son Jesus is His love letter to us. Oh, how he loves you and me so much! He loved us to the cross, on the cross, and as He rose from the grave to go and prepare a place for us. And in His love for us, He promised to come again for us, soon!

*P*RAYER FOR THIS WEEK

*Jesus, thank-you seems like such*
*a small thing to say for taking my sin*
*to the cross. Help me live in such*
*a way that I show that I am always*
*thankful for your sacrifice on Calvary.*
*In Your name, amen.*

# REMNANT

*Once more a remnant of the kingdom of Judah*
*will take root below and bear fruit above.*
*For out of Jerusalem will come a remnant,*
*and out of Mount Zion a band of survivors.*
*The zeal of the* LORD *Almighty will accomplish this.*
ISAIAH 37:31-32

When I started this devotion, I thought it would be interesting to see how many different synonyms there are for the word remnant. According to Thesaurus.com there are thirty-two relevant synonyms for remnant. The top eight are as follows: bit, fragment, particle, piece, remains, residue, shred, vestige. The easiest definition is a small part of something. When I was younger, I thought remnant had to do with carpet and it was cheaper. I am not sure I really understood the deeper biblical meaning until I was an adult.

We as Christians are the remnant of God. We are His light into this dark world. And right now, we are a fragment of His people called to share the gospel and witness to God's work of saving souls. I want to be in the remnant that God brings out to tell the world about His Son Jesus and the gift of salvation and eternal life through Him.

The prophet Isaiah talks about God's remnant of Israel in our theme verse for this week. I believe this was true for Israel three thousand years ago and it has implications for today and the future, because the zeal of the Lord will make this come to pass. There was a remnant then and we as His church are the remnant now. What a privilege and honor to be a part of it!

*P*RAYER FOR THIS WEEK
*Lord God, give us a spirit of boldness*
*to share You with the world.*
*In Jesus's name, amen.*

# IMPATIENTLY PATIENT

*I waited patiently for L*ORD*;*
*he turned to me and heard my cry.*
*He lifted me out of the slimy pit,*
*out of the mud and mire;*
*he set my feet on a rock*
*and gave me a firm place stand.*
*He put a new song in my mouth,*
*a hymn of praise to our God.*
*Many will see and fear the L*ORD
*and put their trust in him.*

PSALM 40:1-3

Hurry up and wait. Good things come to those wait. We live in a microwave society; we don't want to have to wait for anything. Fast food, express appointments, fast-forward through commercials, instant messaging, you get the picture. I miss a slower pace and simpler times, Mayberry time. The Andy Griffith show has always been one of my favorite shows even as a kid but even more so now. I love the episode titled "Man in a Hurry." The story line follows Mr. Tucker, a busy businessman, as his car breaks down on a Sunday in Mayberry. He walks the town and can find no one, because everyone is in church. Gomer is working at Wally's filling station, and he is only allowed to pump gas on Sunday. Mr. Tucker is aggravated and extremely impatient to find that his schedule is at mercy of Mayberry.

We all know there is no urgency in Mayberry, as impatient as he was with everyone, the town of Mayberry taught him a lesson in patience and slowing down wasn't a bad thing at all. Mr. Tucker learned to wait. We are not always the best "wait-ers." God says be patient, but we want our prayers answered now. Yes, He hears our prayers, and our cries to Him. But we must be reminded that His answers will come in His timing not ours, so we wait patiently for Him.

As we saw in our theme verse for this week, David knew about waiting. Will you patiently wait for the Lord?

### 𝒫RAYER FOR THIS WEEK

*Father, help us recognize the opportunities*
*you give us daily to be patient and that patience*
*will help us be more in tune with you. Help us trust*
*Your timing as You answer our prayers.*
*In Jesus's name, amen.*

# WHERE WOULD YOU RATHER BE?

*Better is one in your courts than a thousand elsewhere;*
*I would rather be the doorkeeper in the house*
*of my God than dwell in the tents of the wicked.*

PSALM 84:10

The telephone rang off the hook at work from the time I walked in until I left. It was at the beginning of Covid shutdowns, and we were a long-term care and nursing facility. It was overwhelming trying to keep up with the calls. Families were worried sick about their loved ones, who were so vulnerable. Everyone wanted to talk to the nurses for reports. It was a lot! As with any job there are good and bad days, but Covid felt like bad days on steroids. Honestly, I wanted to be anywhere else but there. Everyone was on edge trying to navigate the shutdowns. Family members were angry because they could no longer visit or because they were not getting return phone calls as fast as they thought they should.

All the protocols coming in daily were on a whole different level too. Personal Protection Equipment and the who, what, where, when, why, and how things were done one day could change just a few days later. One positive thing it did was to bring our facility closer together, like family. Like family we ebbed and flowed, but we were an awesome team.

Just like the psalmist who wrote our theme verse for this week, I would rather spend one day with God, being his hands, and feet in His service, than anywhere else. I knew the families of our patients needed a compassionate voice and a loving tone, offering words of encouragement, understanding, and prayers. That is how I would want to be spoken to, especially if I was worried about my loved one. This might be the one and only time they will have to see the love of God being lived out. What a privilege it is to share Him.

#### Prayer for this week

*Jesus, never let us miss an opportunity*
*to show who You are in our day-to-day lives.*
*In Your name, amen.*

# WHERE WERE YOU?

*Even though I walk through the darkest valley,*
*I will fear no evil, for you are with me;*
*your rod and your staff, they comfort me.*
*Surely your goodness and love*
*will follow me all the days of my life,*
*and I will dwell in the house of the LORD forever.*

PSALM 23:4, 6

Every generation has at least one event that stands out in their memories, and they know exactly where they were when it happened. For my great-grandparents and my grandparents, these events included hearing that the US had entered WWI and WWII, the Wall Street Crash of 1929, hearing that Japan had bombed Pearl Harbor and that an atomic bomb had been dropped on Japan, D-Day, and hearing that the wars had come to an end.

For my parents it was the beginning of the Korean and Vietnam wars, the moon landing, and the assassinations of Martin Luther King Jr. and John F. Kennedy. For my generation it was the fall of the Berlin Wall, the Challenger Space Shuttle tragedy, the ending of the Cold War, the Oklahoma City bombing, and the 9/11 attacks on the World Trade Center twin towers along with the Pentagon and Shanksville, Pennsylvania. These are just to name a few.

I remember exactly where I was when I heard the news of the 9/11 attacks. My mom said the same thing about when Kennedy died. There are some who have said, "I know where I was, but where was God?" God was there in the trenches of every war with every soldier. God was there when Israel became a State. God was there when they landed on the moon. God was there when Martin Luther King Jr. lost his life as part of the Civil Rights Movement. God was in Oklahoma City when the bomb exploded. God was with those on the planes that crashed into the towers and the Pentagon and in Pennsylvania. God was in the stairwells, in elevators, under desks. God was on the phone with loved ones when they called to say their last good-byes and I-love-yous. God was on the 110th floor with those who were trapped. God. Was. There. He was there whispering, "I will *never* leave you nor *forsake* you."

Do you know where else God was? He was in the same place when His Son Jesus was nailed to the cross for your sin and mine. Don't ever think God isn't present during tragedies. He is omniscient, omnipresent, and omnipotent. Let Him comfort you even as you walk through dark valleys.

### $\mathcal{P}$RAYER FOR THIS WEEK

*Precious Father, thank You*
*for Your love and the assurance that*
*You will never leave us nor forsake us.*
*In Jesus's name, amen.*

# ANGELS ON EARTH

*Do not forget to show hospitality to strangers,*
*for by so doing some people have shown hospitality*
*to angels without knowing it.*
HEBREWS 13:2

My oldest daughter, Ashley, was very sick when she was eighteen months old. I was a new mom, with no insurance; so going to the doctor was not cheap. I wanted her to feel better so badly that I started bargaining with God to make my baby better. Give the sickness to me! The doctor examined her and did some labs . . . she had scarlet fever. I was scared. He prescribed a strong, relatively new antibiotic. I took it to the pharmacy to get it filled and was told it was going to cost $150. I said I didn't have that kind of money. I started to cry. I heard a man's voice behind me ask if my daughter needed it, I said, "She does." The man told the cashier he would take care of it with his bill. The pharmacist was going over the directions with me and when I turned around to tell him thank you so much, he was gone. They didn't know who "he" was.

Our youngest daughter, Jordan, was involved in a rollover car accident. It was raining, a car veered into her lane, she swerved to miss it and hit a guide wire attached to a telephone pole. She was scared to death. She couldn't get the car door open! The next thing she knew, a man opened her car door and helped her get out. She was shaken up and banged up but okay. When she went to say thank you to the man he was gone. I asked where the man was, when we got there, so that we could thank him. She said, "Mom, he disappeared."

Angels are all around us, seen and unseen.

$\mathcal{P}$RAYER FOR THIS WEEK
*Father God, thank You for sending*
*Your angels to watch over us.*
*In Jesus's name, amen.*

# CHANGE HAPPENS,
# LIKE IT OR NOT

*Jesus Christ is the same yesterday*
*and today and forever.*
HEBREWS 13:8

Change happens, whether we like it or not, and for some, it is anxiety inducing, stressful, painful, and fearful. It can turn your world upside down. Change for some is exciting, hopeful, adventurous, welcomed, and needed. Funny, how we are all in one of those two groups.

When my dad passed away in 2009 and my mom passed away in 2020, I was forever changed. I felt like an orphan. I did not like change at all then. I am usually up for the adventure.

Some of us like knowing what to expect and the routines we develop. Routine can be comforting. But we can become stagnate without change. We can fight change or roll with it. When we fight it, we are fighting growth that God has placed in our life for a reason or a season. When we roll with it, we experience God's plan without the delays of fighting it. It is something we do not have to fear because God is in control. When I try to control the direction of my life, I run it off in the ditch. Every. Single. Time.

There is someone who never changes. Our verse for this week reminds us that Jesus Christ does *not* change despite the changing circumstances we face.

When change shows up at your door, invite it in and give it a comfortable place to sit like you would an old friend.

*P*RAYER FOR THIS WEEK
*Lord Jesus, may we always have*
*a welcoming spirit for change,*
*to help us grow according to Your will.*
*In Your name, amen.*

# THE FORBIDDEN FRUIT CAN GET YOU IN A JAM

*When tempted, no one should say, "God is tempting me."*
*For God cannot be tempted by evil, nor does he tempt anyone;*
*but each person is tempted when they are dragged*
*away by their own evil desire and enticed. Then,*
*after desire has conceived, it gives birth to sin; and sin,*
*when it is full-grown gives birth to death.*
*Don't be deceived, my dear brothers and sisters.*
JAMES 1:13–16

Twenty years ago, as I was driving past a church one day, I saw this saying for the first time: "The forbidden fruit can get you in a Jam!" I have never forgotten it. It's simple, profound, and to the point. We have all had some type or form of temptation in our lives. For a diabetic, it might be the temptation of a decadent dessert that's loaded with carbs, calories, and sugar. For those who are married, it might be the allure of engaging in an affair. We can all be tempted to jump on the bandwagon of gossip and malicious talk about a friend or family member. Or some are drawn to looking at inappropriate things on the Internet.

Remember this song? "Oh, be careful little eyes what you see, for the Father up above is looking down in love. So be careful little eyes what you see." And there are verses for the mouth, feet, hands, and ears. Again simple, profound, and to the point.

But better than any pithy saying or childhood song, we know we can overcome temptation because Jesus overcame temptation. He was tempted in every way, even as we are tempted. And because he suffered when He was tempted, He promises to help us when we are tempted (Hebrews 2:18; 4:14–16).

While James talks about sin originating inside each of us in our verse for this week, Peter also reminds us that Satan prowls around like a lion looking for someone to devour (1 Peter 5:8) and any of us could be next if we don't run to God when we are tempted. Oh, be careful . . .

### $\mathcal{P}$RAYER FOR THIS WEEK

*Jesus, thank You that we can come*
*with boldness before Your throne of grace*
*to find help in our time or need.*
*Guard our hearts, minds, bodies and souls*
*always with Your loving protection.*
*In Your name, amen.*

# THE LAST CURTAIN CALL

*The curtain of the temple*
*was torn in two from top to bottom.*

MARK 15:38

Have you ever seen a big guy in some of the Strongman competitions that can tear a full phone book in half? It is a novel idea I know for some of the younger generations. This was pre-cellphones, computers, and Internet at your fingertips. "Let your fingers do the walking in the yellow pages"; that was the advertisement for the phone book. It depended on where you lived how thick your phone book could be. Where I lived, the phone book consisted of white and yellow pages combined—white pages for residential listings and yellow pages for business listings. Which made it about three to four inches thick.

In Mark 14:58 Jesus said, "I will destroy this temple made with human hands and in three days will build another, not made with hands." At the time they were not sure what he meant. But we know now that he was referring to his own body. No one understood what Jesus meant. In the temple of Jesus's day there was a curtain that separated God in His Holy Place from sinful man. There are specific descriptions and instructions for this curtain—sixty feet long, thirty feet wide, seventy-two squares joined together. Although we don't know for sure how thick it was, it is believed that it was about four inches thick.

When Jesus died on the cross, He changed *everything*! As Jesus breathed His last breath, the curtain was torn from top to bottom by God. His hands were the only ones that could tear it. He is the ultimate Strongman, able to make a way for us to access God.

Now we are no longer separated from God, because Jesus took our sin upon Himself as He was crucified. If you don't know Jesus as your Lord and Savior, please ask Him to come into your heart today. He's waiting for you, and He will meet you right where you are!

### $\mathscr{P}$RAYER FOR THIS WEEK

*Loving Savior, may we always hear You*
*in our heart that You turned from stone to flesh*
*the moment we asked You to come into it.*
*In Jesus's name, amen.*

# PREPARATIONS

*My Father's house has many rooms;*
*if that were not so, would I have told you*
*that I am going there to prepare a place*
*for you? And if go and prepare a place for you,*
*I will come back and take you to be with me*
*that you also may be where I am.*
*You know the way to the place where I am going.*
JOHN 14:2–4

Whether we are going on a trip, fixing Thanksgiving dinner, going to the grocery store, or having people come and stay with us, we must prepare. Like anything we prepare for, we are usually ready to crash by the end. Preparations are symbols of love, showing that someone took precious time to prepare just for you. Best of all is how much love you feel.

There are preparations going on in the kingdom of God right now that we cannot see, but we know that it is happening. Jesus said so!

John's gospel tells us in this week's Bible passage that Jesus is preparing a place for me! Knowing how much He loves me and the thought that He is excited for me to come to live with Him in His Father's house is overwhelming happiness. Jesus is doing the same for you too! The preparations are in full swing in heaven for our arrival. Let's be ready!

## Prayer for this week

*Jesus, thank You for promising to prepare*
*a place for us in Your Father's house.*
*Help us to continue to prepare for that time too,*
*sharing with others about*
*who You are and how much You love us.*
*In Jesus's name, amen.*

# FORGOTTEN

*Are not five sparrows sold for two pennies?*
*Yet not one of them is forgotten by God.*
*Indeed, the very hairs of your head are all numbered.*
*Don't be afraid; you are worth more than many sparrows.*
LUKE 12:6–7

Have you ever been forgotten? It doesn't feel good; as a matter of fact, it hurts. As kids are having parties for birthdays and they are handing out invitations, everyone gets an invite except you! The excuse: "Oh, I must have left it at home. I'll bring it tomorrow." Tomorrow never comes. I was always excited for Valentine's Day parties at school, and when it came time to exchange our valentines, some of us didn't have as many as others. The excuse: "Sorry, I didn't have enough. I ran out." But ironically, those boxes of valentines had the same number of cards in them, and the teacher would always send home a list of names and the number in each class.

When we feel forgotten as kids, it hurts. And it might hurt worse as an adult, because adults should know better. It still happens, regardless of age. But when tomorrow comes and our friend is looking for us to give us our party invitation or valentine or whatever situation we face as an adult, to let us know we aren't forgotten . . . Wow! It makes us feel wanted and remembered.

As our verse for this week reminds us, God doesn't forget us! His eye is on the sparrow, and I know He's watching over me. I am not forgotten. I am worth more than many sparrows. He even knows the number of the hairs on my head! I am seen, known, and valued.

*P*RAYER FOR THIS WEEK
*Thank You, God, for Your loving
and watchful eye over each one of us,
always. Teach us to be as loving
and compassionate as You are.
In Jesus's name, amen.*

# OUR SHEPHERD

*Suppose one of you has a hundred sheep and
loses one of them. Doesn't he leave the ninety-nine
in the open country and go after the lost sheep
until he finds it? And when he finds it, he joyfully puts it
on his shoulders and goes home. Then he calls his friends
and neighbors together and says, "Rejoice with me;
I have found my lost sheep." I tell you that in the same
way there will be more rejoicing in heaven over
one sinner who repents than over ninety-nine
righteous persons who do not need to repent.*

LUKE 15:4–7

As a kid, did you ever get lost in a large place? I remember walking into a store with an adult and having instant sensory overload. I had already mapped out in my mind the toy aisles, candy aisles, and junk food aisles. I can confidently say I do not remember any other aisles growing up. And our store rules? "You better behave. Don't ask for or touch anything. You stay right next to me and don't wander off. Do you understand me?" "Yes ma'am."

I could not tell you how long it took before, you guessed it, I got lost. Mom was looking at something, and the second she wasn't paying attention, I was gone. I knew right where the toys were, or so I thought. I was so scared when I realized I was lost and so happy when she found me. After we get in trouble, we understand why we are supposed to stay right next to our parents.

When I read Jesus's story in Luke's gospel, I realized that I was the one that was lost. I felt so special that heaven was rejoicing over me when I repented and accepted Jesus. Heaven will do the same thing for you.

### 𝒫RAYER FOR THIS WEEK
*Jesus, thank You for seeking out each lost lamb*
*and giving us the gift of eternal life*
*that only comes through accepting You*
*as our personal Lord and Savior.*
*In Your name, amen.*

# STICKS AND STONES

*With the tongue we praise our Lord and Father,*
*and with it we curse human beings,*
*who have been made in God's likeness.*
*Out of the same mouth come praise and cursing.*
*My brothers and sisters, this should not be.*
*Can both fresh water and salt water flow*
*from the same spring?*

JAMES 3:9–11

Sticks and stones may break my bones, but words will never hurt me . . . said no one ever and meant it. Words do hurt. There is an old Italian saying, "The tongue has no bones, but it can break bones." Ironically, people who we think are winning in life have felt the sticks and stones too. "Throw your stick and stones, throw your bombs and your blows, but you're not gonna break my soul" (Katy Perry). "You will never reach your destination if you stop and throw stones at every dog that barks" (Winston Churchill). "Sticks and stones may break me, but the words you said just tore my heart in two" (Tracy Lawrence).

I don't know about you, but when I was told that "words will never hurt me," I always thought, *You're joking right?* I was teased relentlessly growing up and I can say that those words hurt. And even though it was forty-five years ago, it still feels like it was yesterday. It's hard to forget the way it hurt. I don't think, given the climate of our world right now, that most don't care about words or the effects that they have on our society.

The words of James in this week's passage should make us think twice before we open our mouth to praise then curse. We need to build each other up with our words, not tear each other down. Imagine the moment you are about to let some not-so-nice things come out of your mouth, and just then, Jesus walks up—something to think about. Oh, be careful little mouth what you say, for the Father up above is looking down in love. Oh, be careful little mouth what you say.

#### Prayer for this week
*Jesus, help us to be mindful*
*of the words in our mouths and*
*in our hearts and keep any unwholesome*
*and hurtful talk from our lips.*
*In Your name, amen.*

# UNASHAMED

*For I am not ashamed of the gospel,
because it is the power of God that brings
salvation to everyone who believes:
first to the Jew, then to the Gentile.*

ROMANS 1:16

Living our lives for Christ Jesus calls us to be bold and unashamed. We must be willing to be uncomfortable sometimes, as we step out in faith to share our testimony about our Savior. It can make us nervous to take that first step to share our faith with someone. We also must live our faith as well, through acts of kindness and service, hospitality, prayer, accountability, forgiveness, studying His Word daily, being the face of God to those who do not know Him.

Cassie Bernall was unashamed. Cassie was a beautiful seventeen-year-old girl who was tragically murdered on April 20, 1999. Now you probably do not recognize her name or the date right off, but Cassie was one of fifteen who died that day, including the two gunmen in the Columbine High School massacre.

Cassie went through some rough times with the wrong crowd who lead her down the path of Satanic worship. Her parents got her away from that crowd filed a restraining order against them and they moved. She met a friend who invited her on a youth retreat with church and there she accepted Jesus into her life. On that fateful day, April 20, 1999, when evil walked into the library where Cassie and others were hiding, frightened for their lives, one of the gunmen walked over to the table where she was hiding, her eyes were closed with her hands on both sides of her face as she was praying and was shot. I pray we are as courageous and unashamed as Cassie and countless others who have died for their faith.

$\mathcal{P}$RAYER FOR THIS WEEK
*Loving God, give us a spirit*
*of boldness to share with those around us*
*about Your precious Son, Jesus,*
*and His gift of salvation through His death,*
*burial and resurrection.*
*In Jesus's name, amen.*

# PURIM

*[Mordecai] wrote them to observe the days as days*
*of feasting and joy and giving presents of food*
*to one another and gifts to the poor. . . .*
*The Jews took it on themselves to establish the custom*
*that they and their descendants and all who join them*
*should without fail observe these two days every year.*

ESTHER 9:22, 27

Purim is a Jewish holiday that is celebrated in the spring. It memorializes the survival of the Jews from Haman's plot to kill them all. *Pur*—means "lots," remembering how Haman cast lots to decide what day the Jews were to be slaughtered. (Read the whole story in the book of Esther and about Purim in chapter 9.) Purim is celebrated on the 14th or 15th day of Adar (March).

Purim traditions such as exchanging gifts of food and drink is called *Mishloach Manot*. Donating charitable gifts to the poor and needy is known as *Mattanot LaEvyonim*. Eating the meal of celebration is known as *Se'udat Purim. Kreplach* and *hamantaschen* pastries are triangular and represent the three-cornered hat of Haman.

Haman's plot to kill the Jews was thwarted by Mordecai and Esther. Haman's plan failed and was turned back upon himself. He was impaled for his treason along with his ten sons. Safe to say, you don't mess with the apple of God's eye (see Deuteronomy 32:9–11). For as He "watches over Israel, [He] will neither slumber nor sleep" (Psalm 121:4).

Haman tried. Haman failed. Hitler tried. Hitler failed. Hmmm . . . a pattern? *Always remember God's words: "I will bless those who bless you and whoever curses you I will curse"* (Genesis 12:3).

*Never cease to pray for the peace of Jerusalem!*

## $\mathcal{P}$RAYER FOR THIS WEEK

*Father, thank You for preserving Your people,*
*both the nation of Israel, and Your church.*
*Thank You for loving us as the apple of Your eye.*
*We pray for the peace and blessing of Jerusalem.*
*In Jesus's name, amen.*

# AM I QUALIFIED?

*And he who searches our hearts knows the mind*
*of the Spirit, because the Spirit intercedes*
*for God's people in accordance with the will of God.*
*And we know that in all things God works*
*for the good of those that love him, who have been*
*called according to his purpose.*

ROMANS 8:27-28

When it comes to looking for a job one of the first things we often do is read the job description and qualifications. The next question is "Am I qualified?" Looking for a job is a dreaded task—filling out applications, submitting your résumé, going to interviews and second interviews. And then you still might find out that they feel you're not qualified! Do you ever look at some high-paying jobs that you know you are not qualified for, but try to justify your lack of experience?

> Fortune 500 company seeks candidate for CEO position. Must have master's degree, 25 years of experience, excellent communication skills, de-escalation, negotiation, organizational skills, ability to delegate tasks with clear instructions, ability to multitask required, etc. Qualified candidates only.

After reading a job description like this, I realized that I have been selling myself short all these years! A CEO job is also a *mom* job! I could have been making the big bucks!

It is easy to say "I am not qualified" for something that is out of our comfort zone at our church, community, workplace, or even home. God will call us out of that safe space to use the most unlikely and unqualified people according to His will to do extraordinary things. Look at, Moses, Jonah, David, Esther, Joseph, John the Baptist, Noah, Mary Magdalen, Zacchaeus, Peter, Paul and the list goes on.

God doesn't call the qualified; God qualifies the called. And, as we saw in this week's theme verse, we are all called according to God's purposes.

Don't be afraid to answer the call and God will do the rest!

### 𝒫RAYER FOR THIS WEEK

*Father God, move us*
*when we are afraid to move.*
*Help us to answer Your call to*
*obey and trust You*
*to equip us for the tasks ahead.*
*In Jesus's name, amen.*

# THE FAMILY TEN BOOM

*Who shall separate us from the love of Christ?*
*Shall trouble or hardship or persecution or famine*
*or nakedness or danger or sword? As it is written:*
*"For your sake we face death all day long;*
*we are considered as sheep to be slaughtered."*
*No, in all these things we are more than conquerors*
*through him who loved us.*
ROMANS 8:37

Have you ever read the book "The Hiding Place"? It is about a family who was a part of the Dutch resistance during WWII and used the family's watchmaking store as a front in Haarlem, Netherlands, near Amsterdam. Corrie, her sister Betsie, her father Casper, along with other family members, were able to hide Jews fleeing Nazi persecution in a hidden wall (The Hiding Place). At the risk of their own safety, they helped eight hundred Jews and other refugees over the course of two years before the ten Boom family was betrayed and sent to concentration camps.

In 1944 the family was sent to prison. Corrie and Betsie were sent to Ravensbruck concentration camp for women. Sadly, Casper became sick while he was in prison and died in a hospital hallway ten days after his arrest. The sisters were in an overcrowded bunkhouse infested with lice and fleas; Corrie was frustrated about the miserable conditions. Betsie reminded her that because of that they could witness to the women in their bunkhouse, pray with them, encourage them, and read the Bible with them. Those guards wouldn't come in, since they knew the lice and fleas would jump on them too! *Wow.*

Thankful for fleas and lice so they could share the love of God. Could I be so bold, so thankful in those circumstances? Could you? I think I would be caught up in self-pity and bitterness over the situation, thinking that God might have forgotten what we had been doing in "the hiding place." But, no, He didn't forget. Corrie and her sister were exactly where God placed them.

As our theme verse for the week reminds us, *nothing* can separate us from the love of God. So let's focus on His will, not our will; His plan, not our plan; His thoughts, not our thoughts; His ways, not our ways.

### $\mathscr{P}$RAYER FOR TODAY

*Father God, thank You for the loving plan*
*You have for my life. Help me to see You*
*in every situation, still fulfilling Your purposes.*
*In Jesus's name, amen.*

# WHO MADE ME A JUDGE?

*Do not judge, and you will not be judged.*
*Do not condemn and you will not be condemned.*
*Forgive, and you will be forgiven.*
LUKE 6:37

Older generations have some great sayings like these:

- Don't put the cart before the horse.
- Don't count your chickens before they hatch.
- Pretty is as pretty does.
- You'll catch more flies with honey than vinegar.
- Too many cooks spoil the gravy.
- Don't judge a book by its cover.
- There's no use crying over spilt milk.
- People in glass houses shouldn't throw stones.
- You're the bee's knees.
- Your daddy ain't no glass maker.

I know you have probably heard all of these at some point in your life. One of my favorites is, don't judge a book by its cover. I have been

guilty of judging more than once. I learned a powerful lesson about judging someone because of how they looked.

Several years ago, my oldest daughter worked at a popular restaurant that we frequented often, and she made friends there. One friend was very different. He was Goth in appearance, and I didn't want to sit in his section at all because of this. She told me how nice he was, and that I should talk to him and sit in his section . . . Nope! Well, guess what happened the next time I was there, which just happened to be after church. His section had the only available tables. My daughter was right! He was the nicest guy ever, really. We got to know him, and we sat in his section every time. We met his girlfriend as well; she was very sweet. They left their jobs and went on a competitive reality show and every Sunday night they had a watch party at a pizza place, and they invited us to come. We went and had a good time. They sat with us instead of their fans and friends.

That was one of the most powerful lessons I have ever learned, and I am so glad I did.

"You love. I judge, God."

*P*RAYER FOR TODAY
*Father God, remind us to see people*
*through Your eyes and not our own.*
*In Jesus's name, amen.*

# F.R.O.G.

*Teach me your way, L*ORD,
*that I may rely on your faithfulness;*
*give me an undivided heart,*
*that I may fear your name. I will praise you,*
*Lord my God, with all my heart;*
*I will glorify your name forever.*

PSALM 86:11-12

My husband and I lived in Charleston, South Carolina, for almost three years and while living there I made precious lifelong friends. My tribe. I was at my friend's house and noticed little frogs on her window ledge inside her kitchen. When I asked her about them, she shared that in preparation for a sermon our minister was doing, he had asked her to get some small frogs that they could hand out afterward. Not really understanding what this was about, I asked what the sermon had to do with frogs. She explained that the sermon was going to be about what the letters stand for—**F**ully **R**ely **O**n **G**od or F.R.O.G. I loved it from the moment she told me the meaning.

When I started working at a nursing home, I quickly grew to love all my coworkers. For my first Christmas there I wanted to get everyone something, but it would have to be something that wasn't very expensive. So . . . what could I buy that didn't cost a lot but would be a good gift for everyone? I thought about it for a couple of days, and finally, I knew exactly what to get each one . . . a small frog. The most precious gift I could give anyone is God. And this seemed to be a way to share God and His message. So, I ordered a hundred small plastic frogs and gave one to each person along with the meaning behind F.R.O.G. They loved their frogs and what they stood for!

So, the next time you see a little frog or a big frog, remember to F.R.O.G.—FULLY RELY ON GOD! Happy Frog-ing!

## *P*RAYER FOR TODAY

*Lord God, help us to fully rely on You always.*
*In Jesus's name, amen.*

# PASS THE SALT

*You are the salt of the earth. But if the salt
loses its saltiness, how can it be made salty again?
It is no longer good for anything,
except to be thrown out and trampled underfoot.*
MATTHEW 5:13

When I was young, I would sneak the saltshaker off the table all the time. Why? Because I love the taste of salt! I would (as gross as this is) lick the palm of my hand, shake salt all over it and, well, lick it off. Yes, I know, gross. I would put salt on everything to the point my mom had to oversee the saltshaker for a while. I would seemingly get in trouble over it everywhere I went. Even at my great grandparents' house. We went there every Sunday for dinner.

My Mamaw and Papaw Dalton lived in the country in Breckenridge County, Kentucky in a town called Hardinsburg. They had the coolest house on the main road, with a big ol' porch, chairs, and a glider. I loved that house as a kid! I can still remember what it smelled like there—earthy outside but warm and comforting inside. Some of my best memories growing up were in the country. Our family was always there . . . cousins, aunts, uncles. I miss it more than I ever thought I would as a kid. It is sad that many kids do not understand the simpler way of life in the country.

Now we all know salt is used in the country for an abundance of things like curing meat, canning vegetables, as a salt lick for animals, healing wounds, and, of course, everyday cooking. Never a shortage of it. I knew mom did not control the shaker at Mamaw's because it was not her shaker to control, or so I thought. But I got caught red-handed with it and got into trouble. I heard my mom telling my great-grandparents and my grandmother about how I was eating salt all the time. They also knew I was listening because the windows were all open.

I heard something that scared me so bad I did not touch salt for a long time.

As my mom is telling them about my salt problem my great-grand-daddy said, "Well, I guess when she eats enough salt and goes to bed, she'll turn into a piece of bacon. Then the only thing left to do will be to fry her up for breakfast!" I was scared! But guess what? I left the salt alone for a long time.

What happens if you eat a lot of salt? It is not long before you become very thirsty, and you want to drink. As our theme verse for this week reminds us, the things of this world will never satisfy. But Jesus is the Living Water that can solely quench our thirst.

When you look at salt or a saltshaker, let it be a reminder to be thirsty for the Living Water—Jesus. Thirst for a closer relationship with Him.

### $\mathcal{P}$RAYER FOR THE WEEK

*Jesus, thank You for sustaining us*
*with the only spiritual water and*
*bread we will ever need.*
*In Jesus's name, amen.*

# DON'T JUST STAND THERE, SHUT UP!

*Words from the mouth of the wise are gracious,*
*but fools are consumed by their own lips.*

ECCLESIASTES 10:12

We have five children between my husband, Dale, and myself. He has a daughter and son from a previous marriage. I have two daughters from a previous marriage, and we have one daughter together. My poor husband was swimming in the estrogen ocean with five females in one house. Yes, the fifth female was my husband's mom who moved in with us as well. She was a wonderful mother-in-law and I loved her dearly.

Having three daughters under one roof, guess what I discovered? God has a sense of humor! I however did not find the humor in it especially when the teenage years hit! Oy Vey! Now since I was a kid, I had been hearing my mom tell me many times a day the infamous mother's curse: "I hope you have kids that act just exactly the way you do, only WORSE". Pfffttt, mothers curse buh-loney . . . I know you know where I'm going next!

The curse is real y'all! Man, I got it back in spades and then some. I know that this is gonna come as a big surprise to some mommas and daddy's but did y'all know teenagers know *everything*?! Well, they do according to our girls. They thought we were dumb parents, so how could we possibly know more than they do? Let me get a towel to clean up the drops of sarcasm that last sentence was dripping with as I laugh.

I would ask them if they had a headache. And they would say no, why? My response always got an eyeroll. "I'm sorry, I just assumed you must since the knowledge fairy came and inserted all the knowledge in the world into your little brain!" Have you ever heard the saying, "Never miss an opportunity to shut up"? I would add to that "and listen." Smart people, wise people know when to do both.

Early in Solomon's rule as king of Israel, God came to him in the night and said, "Ask for whatever you want me to give you." Though Solomon was still young, he asked for wisdom. I'm sure I would have asked for something lame, but God was molding Solomon, so he gave him just what he asked for, plus many blessings beside. Solomon did become a wise man and ruler, and we saw a sample of that in this week's verse.

Solomon wrote over three thousand proverbs. There are approximately 915 in Proverbs. "Wisdom is more precious than rubies, and nothing you desire can compare with her" (Proverbs 8:11). That sums it up! Wisdom is priceless and worth more than we could pay for it. Never be afraid to pray for wisdom. It's a smart thing to do!

### $\mathcal{P}$RAYER FOR TODAY

*Jesus, please give me wisdom in all I do and say*
*and close my mouth when it's wise to do so.*
*In Your name, amen.*

# EVERY VILLAGE NEEDS A TRIBE . . .
# AND ONE IDIOT

*A friend loves at all times, and a brother*
*is born for a time of adversity.*
PROVERBS 17:17

Do you have a BFF, BFFEL, TPIAP, BFFTLL, FTTE? I know you are won-dering if this is a secret code. All right campers get your secret decoder pin out . . . (No, it's not a crummy commercial telling you to be sure to drink your Ovaltine! Sorry, I couldn't resist. *A Christmas Story* is one of my favorite movies!)

- BFF = best friends forever
- BFFEL = best friends for everlasting life
- TPIAP = two peas in a pod
- BFFTLL = best friends for totally like life (so '80s)
- FTTE = friends 'til the end

How many friends like this do you have or consider like this?

I never thought about what friendships would look like as an adult or what they would mean to me as an adult. I met Andrea 30 years ago when she worked as the desk clerk in the police station, and I would take her favorite drink HI-C Pink Lemonade and hang out with her. We became family instantly and have been ever since. I met Tina, twenty-two years ago during a hard time. She was going through a divorce. Been there, done that, got the T-shirt. We were in the same Sunday school class. I asked her if she'd like to walk the next day, and the rest, they say is history!

We watched our kids grow up together during the good times and the bad, through school, then college, cancer, deaths, surgeries, accidents, weddings, everything . . . together. We had already gone through my cancer surgery in August of 2013. Then in December my husband had to have a heart cath. The doctor found that he had three blocked arteries at 70%, 80%, and 90%. They stinted two of them. He is the absolute love of my life and the thought of something happening to him scared me.

He was in law enforcement for over thirty-five years and had been a police officer in our city department for twenty-eight years at the time of his retirement in 2017. I didn't want us to live a life of regret, talking about the things we want to do in life but never doing them.

Over the years we had vacationed in Charleston, South Carolina. One of my most favorite places. When we would get there on vacation, we never wanted to leave. There was something special about being there. We would talk about making it a staycation but that's all it was, talk.

One day while we were there, it happened. We seriously talked about moving, and he was on board with it. Truth be told, I almost fell over.

We started the process. It was exciting and nerve-racking. Our house sold three days after we put it on the market, so we were able to put a contract on a brand-new house. As we started packing and it became more and more real—we were really doing this! I was sad about leaving and excited about our next chapter. We said our good-byes, sad to leave and eager to go.

We got moved in and learned that one of next-door neighbors had just moved in a month before us, and they were from the same city as us and another neighbor had the same last name as one of our beloved neighbors back home. Such a God thing. I would say, what are the odds, but there are no odds with God. We found a church we loved four months later.

Again, such a God thing. We clicked. I was happy to have a group of friends so early on. I loved these ladies and being a part of their circle.

God knew I needed these friendships in South Carolina. As time went on, we developed a sisterhood, a Tribe. It was wonderful to pray together and for each other, to study together, and to spend time together. They eventually become the kind of friends who are a part of who you are—always there to cheer you on, to lift you up, to tell you when you're being an idiot, to love on you in spite of your flaws or when you're not very lovable, willing to stand up with you and for you.

We moved back home two and a half years later. My mom had passed away. Three months later my mother-in-law passed away. We had a new grandson. It was time to come home.

I hope, wherever you go, you find your BFF, your bestie, or your Tribe. No Regrets!

Thank you to my Tribe, my Village, and whoever's turn it is to be the idiot. S,D,D,D,A,MA.

### $\mathscr{P}$RAYER FOR THIS WEEK
*Lord God, thank You for loving us and*
*surrounding us with those You have placed in our*
*lives according to Your will and purpose.*
*In Jesus's name, amen.*

# LIFEGUARD

*"Lord, if it's you," Peter replied,*
*"tell me to come to you on the water."*
*"Come," he said. Then Peter got down out of the boat,*
*walked on the water and came toward Jesus.*
*But when he saw the wind, he was afraid and,*
*beginning to sink, cried out, "Lord, save me!"*
*Immediately Jesus reached out his hand*
*and caught him. "You of little faith," he said,*
*"why did you doubt?"*

MATTHEW 14:28-31

My mom had a terrible fear of large bodies of water. We went to Florida one time when I was very young. I remember sitting in the sand, waves washing over me as I tasted the salty water. I wanted my mom to take us in the water. Her answer was *no!* She was afraid of drowning. She liked water if she was sitting in lounge chair looking at it. I couldn't swim either, but I enjoyed being in the water anytime we could go.

Fast-forward to when I was a teenager, I went to stay with my cousins for a few weeks and guess what? They weren't far from a large lake. I was excited to go on the weekends. We went to Rough River Lake (odd name, isn't it?). While we were there, I wanted to go out a little further, but I started to get a little scared. My cousin said he would take me out there, he piggybacked me out into the water and then he threw my arms off and said, "Sink or swim!" I learned how to swim that day by listening to the instructions he gave me.

Whenever you feel like you are drowning in the sea of life and you cannot keep your head above water, don't be afraid! Remember the story of Peter on the water with Jesus and that your *Lifeguard* walks on water! Don't ever doubt that He will save you!

## $\mathcal{P}$RAYER FOR TODAY

*Jesus, thank You for Your saving grace*
*every day, especially since I don't deserve it.*
*Help me to keep my eyes on You,*
*even when I am afraid.*
*In Your precious name, amen.*

# TREASURED AND PONDERED

*Mary treasured up all these things*
*and pondered them in her heart.*

LUKE 2:19

As the mom of three beautiful daughters, there are a lot of things I have treasured from them throughout their childhood traced handprint ornaments, turkeys and butterflies; coloring pictures; clay art projects; leaves pressed in wax paper; writing projects in middle school and high school. As parents we always want to keep everything, but realistically, we can't. I saved some special things from each that have been given back to them now that they are adults. But some things I have treasured and pondered in my heart—when another adult would say how well behaved they had been or that she had been so helpful when she was with them; or when a teacher would say how proud they were of the effort they had put forth after getting off to a rocky start or how great they had been at being a peer tutor to special needs students.

I am so very proud of all three. They each have carved their own way in life; even when it was rough, they did it. When it wasn't easy all the time, they did it. When they wanted to quit, they didn't. I wouldn't let them. I am their biggest cheerleader. They are my treasures.

In two different places in Luke 2 we read that Mary treasured and pondered things in her heart that were said to her about Jesus. When the shepherds came to see the Messiah wrapped in cloths and lying in a manger, they told Mary and Joseph all that the angel had told them, and "Mary treasured up all these things and pondered them in her heart" (v. 19). And years later, when Joseph and Mary found that Jesus wasn't with them when they left Jerusalem, they went back to Jerusalem to look for him. After finding Him in the temple, Jesus asked, "Why were you searching for me? . . . Didn't you know I had to be in my Father's house?" The text goes on to say, "They did not understand what he was saying to them. Then he went down to Nazareth with them and was obedient to them. But his mother treasured all these things in her heart" (vv. 49–51).

There is a scene in the *Passion of the Christ* when Jesus falls, carrying the cross. Mary sees him still as a child falling and, being his mother, runs to comfort him and hold him. She had the same heart and love for Jesus as her child and for Jesus, the Son of God who would bring salvation through His death and resurrection.

Mary was favored among women. She gave birth to the Savior of world. She was a mother who loved her child.

### *P*RAYER FOR THIS WEEK

*Father, thank You for the love of mothers that gives*
*protection and comfort in the ups and downs*
*that this life can throw at us. Help us remember*
*that this maternal love is part of Your image,*
*and You want to shelter us under Your wings!*
*In Jesus's name, amen.*

# JUST DESERTS

*For the LORD has a day of vengeance,*
*a year of retribution, to uphold Zion's cause.*

ISAIAH 34:8

Have you ever wanted to exact revenge in exactly the way you see fit for the person or persons that deserved it? Give them their "just deserts." Now when I was younger, I felt I should get my "just desserts" every day, I deserved an extra serving of cake, pie, ice cream, candy, or whatever was being doled out. Why? Because I thought I deserved sweet treats, until I learned that the phrase "just deserts" didn't have anything to do with extra cake. Instead, based on an old spelling, it means "the punishment that one deserves."

Vengeance is a scary sounding word, and its meaning is just as scary. The New Oxford American Dictionary definition is "punishment inflicted or retribution exacted for an injury or a wrong."

Adolf Hitler. Jozef Stalin. Benito Mussolini. Saddam Hussein. Idi Amin. Vladimir Lenin. Mao Zedong. Genghis Khan. Kim Il Sung. Pol Pot. Hideki Tojo. Ho Chi Minh. Hirohito. Nicolae Ceausescu. Johnny Jihad. These are some of the worst of the worst, and sadly, the list is much longer than these. Should they be given their just deserts? Yes, but not by us. One of the hardest things I have ever been challenged to do from the pulpit was to pray for leaders and terrorists like these. Even though most of them are dead, someone always steps in to replace them, usually with the same ideas and beliefs.

The struggle was real! I didn't want to pray for terrorists, dictators, and extremists who hate us, or anyone who didn't believe same way I did. I thought, *they don't deserve my prayers.* I wanted to exact the "just deserts" prayers, thinking that they don't belong in my heaven. God reminded me, "You love and pray. I judge and it is mine to repay." See, I run it off into the ditch every time I think my way is right.

As Isaiah says, in our theme verse, God will take care of it just as He said He will. I don't want those feelings to become a stumbling block for me or you. In reality, we should get our just deserts too, but Jesus took them instead.

*P*RAYER FOR THIS WEEK
*God of love, thank You for the gift of Jesus*
*and that when we look at the cross, we are reminded*
*that He willingly took what we deserved. Help us to be*
*just as forgiving and compassionate as You are.*
*In Your name, amen.*

# CAN'T NEVER DID NOTHIN'

*I can do all things through [Christ] who gives me strength.*
PHILIPPIANS 4:13

I can't do this. I can't do that. I can't. . . . I think "can't" should be taken out of our vocabulary. My Mamaw would say, "Can't never did nothin'. You can do anything." When our kids were young, they had no issue with dragging out all their toys to wreck a clean room. The problem came when these dreaded words: "It's time to clean up." Nooo! Five more minutes was the response and so the bargaining would begin. Can I do it tomorrow? No. Can I do it when I get home from school? No. Can I go outside and play with my friends and then I will? No.

Ironically, when this happened, a strange phenomenon would take place in their bodies. It's called Meltos Skeletonitis, which in layman's terms means the skeletal system vanishes and all that's left is the puddle of a child lying on the floor. This renders them completely unable to clean up, which happens after "I can't" is uttered. This phenomenon doesn't last very long when the offer of help is presented. It's a miracle how fast they can stand and help. I would ask, "If I didn't make the mess, why am I helping to clean it up?" Answer, because you love me.

According to our theme verse, we never have to say "can't" again, because we "*can*" with Christ Jesus. Whenever can't creeps in, remember what my Mamaw said, "Can't never did nothin'," but you can do everything through Christ who gives you the strength!

### ℘RAYER FOR THIS WEEK
*Jesus, You love me, this I know,*
*for the Bible tells me so.*
*Little ones to You belong;*
*they are weak, but You are strong.*
*In Your name, amen.*